INFERTILE WOMAN

OVERCOMING THE IMPOSSIBLE

STACY WILLIAMS

Copyright © 2023 Stacy Williams
All rights reserved. NO part of this book may be reproduced, transmitted, duplicated, reverse engineered, stored in any informational storage retrieval by means of electronic, or mechanical, WITHOUT the AUTHOR PERMISSION.
ISBN: 979-8-9881748-1-3

DEDICATION

I dedicate this book to my daughter Mireya, which means miracle, and a true miracle she is. She came at a point in my life where I felt less than, unworthy, and the word "NO" seems to be all I heard and knew. Mireya taught me the true meaning of belief, faith, and standing on the word. This book was written to encourage those that are battling infertility to keep pushing. If God did it for me, he can do it for you! All you must do is believe. Keep your heart, eyes, and mind on things that are good. God's not through with you yet. You can defeat the battle with infertility through prayer and meditation, seeking counseling, forgiveness, weight loss, and gratitude.

Another thing that helped me along this journey was a wonderful team of doctors that would listen to me. No one knows your body better than you. You are your advocate and if you have doctors that refuse to listen to your wishes and concerns, you may want to do your research and look for a provider that will listen to you. I leave you with this You can have what you say. Mark 11:23, I tell you the truth, you can say to this mountain, 'May you be lifted up and thrown into the sea,' and it will happen. But you must really believe it will happen and have no doubt in your heart. Remember life and death lie in the tongue.

You got this! I am rooting and praying for you, and your success story!

CONTENTS

Introduction

Chapter 1: Prayer and Meditation: Finding Peace

Chapter 2: Counseling Helps Piece the Puzzle Together

Chapter 3: Forgiveness Make Room For Blessings

Chapter 4: Gratitude is Contagious

Chapter 5: Weight Loss is a Must

Chapter 6: It Did Not Happen Overnight

Introduction

Infertility is a physical and emotional struggle for women who want to have children. There are options available to help you with your fertility - from drug treatments, in vitro fertilization, and adoption. Talk to your doctor about what's best for you and take care of your mental health by seeking support from partners, family members and other women dealing with infertility or who have had a child through medical interventions, such as IVF.

Infertile simply means not having the ability to reproduce. You can become infertile in any area of your life. Whether it's in your finances, health, relationships, mind, and body. This book will discuss infertility in the body. I will share in this book experiences from my journey dealing with infertility. I would like to define infertility as it relates to a woman's body as being unsuccessful in getting pregnant and or the inability to stay pregnant after frequently trying for a year. The main symptom that may suggest that a woman is infertile is irregular menstrual cycles.

 Irregular menstrual cycles occurs when the female is experiencing too long, too short, and or absent cycles. They may also experience breakthrough bleeding. This is where a woman bleed or spot in between periods. Causes of infertility can be from hormone imbalances, fallopian tube damage or blockage, cervical and uterine issues, endometriosis, and poly cystic ovarian syndrome (PCOS).

 However, I am dealing with infertility because of a condition known as Poly Cystic Ovarian Syndrome, also known as (PCOS), which affects my cycles and weight. After getting a good understanding of myself, I have always dealt with irregular cycles since the age of puberty. It wasn't until the age of 25 that I was diagnosed with this condition and told that I would never experience motherhood. It is a very tough reality. At the age of 29, I suffered a miscarriage. After undergoing exploratory surgery, the doctors found polyps in my uterus, which prevented the egg from attaching to the uterus, leading to miscarriage. By age 31, I was pregnant for a second time, "oh boy" I was overjoyed! But having asthma and PCOS while pregnant made my pregnancy very challenging. If I may be open and honest with you all; some of the challenges, I experienced during this pregnancy included, three threaten miscarriages, placenta Previa, having a cycle the full 9-months of the pregnancy, experiencing several asthma attacks, suffering several false labors, and being placed on bedrest majority of my pregnancy. With all of life's challenges I can now say through close monitoring by my care team, I was able to carry my baby full-term and deliver via C-section as a Christmas gift. She was born days before Christmas. Now I am enjoying my baby and celebrating Christmas. By age 33 I faced another trauma. I was pregnant for the third time and things got a little bit real. It quickly became a life-and-death situation. I thought I was having an irregular cycle but came to find out I was miscarrying. I found out I was pregnant ectopically and rushed into surgery.

An ectopic pregnancy is a pregnancy in which the embryo develops outside the uterus. In my case, the embryo had planted itself in my fallopian tube. During surgery, my doctor removed the embryo and my fallopian tube. This left me with so much pain not just in my body, but in my heart. I was filled with all types of emotions. It is assumed that once you give birth, infertility goes away. This way of thinking is so incorrect. There is no cure for infertility or PCOS. The cause is unknown, and it does not go away because someone successfully conceives and gives birth. Just because there is no cure, and the cause is unknown does not mean you cannot cope or survive this difficult battle.

This book will explain the strategies I took to overcome the impossible situations that were happening in my life. My prayer is for this book to guide you through your infertility journey by providing you with basic principles to weather the storms that life may bring and remind you that greatness is in you!

Chapter 1: Prayer and Meditation: Finding Peace

Prayer and meditation are powerful tools that I used to save my life. It gave me a way to escape all the crazy things that were going on in my life from divorce to dealing with infertility, and self-development. After spending time in prayer, I would have a sense of release. Praying allows a person to release and become free of all the things that are troubling you, by releasing the happy hormones that the body produces. Doing these two things would allow me to be real with myself and real with God. It was the only time I could shed the layers that I would put on every day just to interact with the world. I put on a mask daily, so people wouldn't know just how much hurt I was feeling, how much anger was balled up, and how I was growing bitter. Prayer and meditation are the best things that anyone can do when faced with challenges, bad news, and when they feel lost. It allows you to hear from the holy spirit and tap into the subconscious mind. Prayer and meditation utilize both your speaking and listening skills. Prayer is a form of communication with God. Through prayer you make your requests known by giving him all your problems, burdens, and worries. Through mediation you activate your listening skills. This step is especially important. While meditating you activate the power of the holy spirit, who is your everyday guide. He will guide you to the answers that you are seeking. You must be open to receiving and be ok with the answer you receive. Knowing this is critical because we always pray for an answer but are not ok when we get those answers. God don't always give us what we want because what we want may not always be good, healthy, or beneficial to us.

Therefore, the answer you receive will most likely be what you need. God knows all and sees all. He knows what we need before we know what we need. He knows that the answer he provides is a need that we didn't know we had, and it is meeting that need, which is ultimately satisfying our wants.

On the other hand, we tend to shut down after bad news or when we are feeling hopeless and helpless. I know this very well. I felt helplessness and hopelessness while sitting in my car, closet, and bathroom floor, crying my eyes out, begging, and pleading for God to do the impossible in my body and my life. But even at this point, when questioning and wondering why everything bad happens to you and begging for miracles, you must remember that God is all powerful, and you were called for a time such as this. He knows your future because he has a plan for your life. He didn't leave out a chapter of your life story without having a plan. Meditating on God's words and promises can allow you to view things from all perspectives; the doctors, yours, and God. Every day I would cry, I would wake up feeling hopeless, and less than a woman, and worthless, feeling like it was the end of the world, and that nothing could go right for me because I was in such a low place mentally, physically, financially, and emotionally, from the divorce and finding out the reason for the divorce, while still angry about being an barren woman.

    This anger led me to do what I thought any other person would have done. Like, get a hobby or join a club to occupy my time, and so I got a trainer; that's right, a trainer! I needed to take this balled-up anger out on someone or some- thing The more I prayed, the more I trained. I loved the positive feeling that I was getting from doing both. While at the gym I would zone out and meditate on my future and what it would look like having the things to come to pass that I had been praying for. Such as getting pregnant. I am now seeing physical results from working out, and everything was looking up for me and I was losing weight so, I thought to myself I should be able to get pregnant now. "Oh, boy" was I wrong. It didn't happen that way. Things didn't go as planned. Doctors said if I lose some weight, it would be easier to become pregnant. I changed the way I ate, and I worked out more and more and more, but experiencing the joys of becoming pregnant wasn't working in my favor.

Of course, being a woman that is barren you don't want to hear pray about it, you want to hear I got a solution, and or you are pregnant! But the truth is all I heard from everyone is to pray about it. At some point, I had prayed and cried so much that I didn't even have the energy to pray anymore. I felt like I had got on God nerves from all the crying and praying I was doing. By now I realize the doctors are not in control, I was not in control, and the one person who was in control, who could work out a miracle I didn't even want to talk to him anymore. But at the end of the day what else is there to do? There was nothing else to do but to keep going to God in prayer. I prayed until tears started to fall from my eyes. I prayed until I felt relief, I prayed until I felt comfort and strength. The more I prayed the more I felt peace, and the more I was able to make it through the day without being upset, especially when seeing other mothers. The more I prayed the more I was able to think clearly and realized I was already a mom. A mom too many. I may not have given birth to these babies physically, but these were my babies and that's all I needed at that time. Through prayer and meditation, God was able to reveal to me the blessings that were right in front of me and that's when I started to enjoy life more and enjoy it with the kids God had placed in my life. Such as my nieces, nephews, and God-babies, I love and care for these babies as if they are my own.

    As I started to grow with God, in my faith, and patience I learned how powerful prayers can be. I also learned how important it is to wait on God's timing. He knows exactly what we need before we need it. In God's timing, I got my reward, a baby of my own. Mireya came at a time in my life when I had made peace with my past and knew how to pray my way through good and bad times. With her, I got exactly what I prayed for. The journey of pregnancy was hard and stressful, but I was able to successfully carry full-term. It was prayer and meditation that gave me peace, hope, and joy during all the chaos that was going on around me. Day in and day out I meditated on (Jeremiah 29: 11, I alone know the plans I have for you, plans to bring you prosperity and not a disaster, plans to bring about the future you hope for. (GNT). God words are true, faith without works is dead (James 2:17). The same goes for works without faith is dead. In the beginning, I was putting in the work, but I had no faith. I was working out, eating right, and doing everything the doctor had asked but I wasn't getting the results I was praying for. Why? Because doubt and fear were still living in my heart. I said I had faith and I believed but deep down I was still doubting and believing that I could not because that's what I was listening to. So, it did not happen. The Bible says faith comes by hearing and hearing the word. I had to choose the things I lend an ear to, because the more I heard or listened to someone tell me I could not, or I would not, I started to believe that. That's why day in and day out I had to meditate on God's words and promises, so I could build my faith and make my prayers more effective. I was then able to walk by faith and not by sight. Now, my daughter asks every day if she can have a sibling. I respond with yes, let's go

Another thing I learnt while on this journey is, I had to be specific in my requests that I made known to God. I am believing God that even with one Fallopian tube, PCOS, and old age; I will birth another child. He did it before, I know he can do it again. You must believe that you are a walking, talking, miracle, sign, and wonder.

I know I talked about meditating on God's word and listen for the answer, well let me be the tell you warn you, when it's your first time meditating the silence will become so loud. Your brain will wonder and at that very moment you will start to remember all the things you should or want to be doing. But it won't be like this every time you go before the lord. This will be frustrating in the beginning but don't give up, try, and try again until you silence the thoughts that are in your head. As I said before, eventually you will get be a silence the noise around you and create a peaceful quiet space.

It's not easy silencing your thoughts if it's your first time meditating but it will happen if you stay focused. I remember the first time I tried meditating; I was sitting in my closet and for the life of me I could not focus on hearing God or the scripture that I had just finished reading. As I sat there in silence trying to meditate my mind started to wonder. I started to think about what I was going to cook for dinner, what bill I needed to pay, and other silly things like, changing my room around, and going shopping. Basically, all the things that I was not thinking about prior to getting into a place of meditation. It took me a full seven days to get to a place where I could meditate and silence the thoughts that were always loud in my head.

The first thing you must do to effectively meditate and spend time with God is to create a safe space. This space is a place that you can be the most vulnerable with God, you can share your innermost wants, thoughts, desire, hurt, and pain. This safe place can be your closet, bedroom, bathroom, car, and even a quiet space at work. You just want to make sure that this place is not noisy and has little to no traffic, meaning there's no interruptions. Also, make sure you have good lighting. Nothing too bright but not too dark either. Lighting just right, in case you need to read or write. Next, you want to work on quieting those thoughts that will arise when it's your first time practicing the art of meditation. What helped me to silence those thoughts is repeating positive affirmations to myself in my head. Silently, I would say to myself, I have the power to control my thoughts, my mind is silent. I would continue to say this until my thoughts would go silent and I could hear the voice of God. I made sure that I would meditate at the same time daily. It helps not only to develop a habit in prioritizing God, but it trains your mind and shows your brain that you control your thoughts, and your thoughts does not control you. Once I grasped the process of shutting down my thoughts and making my space silence, I then add meditating sounds to my sessions, to keep me in a place of focus and to keep my mind stay on the task at hand. I would some days use the sound of flowing water (i.e., waves, rivers, waterfalls, and rain.) I would sometimes play other sounds like instrumental music or other soft sounds, that will help carry my mind somewhere else.

Lastly, meditation is a practice highly used to reduce stress. Once you get the hang of meditation and can effectively utilize this practice you will start to notice that you are able to better manage your stress. Also, can have more than one safe place, just make sure it brings you peace and joy.

Prayer: Father, I thank you for my life and the body that you have given me. I thank you for giving me the future that I hope for, and I ask that your will be done on earth as it is in heaven. Strengthen me to be okay with the answer you provide. for your will to manifest in my life and to silence every thought that comes to steal my focus during meditation. is my life. My heart's desire is to one day become someone's mother here on earth however you see fit. Bless me oh Lord and my answer is forever yes and Amen. In Jesus' name Amen!

Self-Reflection Questions

1. What amount of time do you spend praying and/or meditating? Why?_____
_____
_____
_____
_____
_____
_____

2. How do you feel after praying and or meditating?_____
_____
_____
_____
_____
_____

3. How do you set the atmosphere for prayer and or meditation?
_____
_____
_____
_____
_____
_____

My Time with God

My yoke is easy and my burden is light!
Matthew 11:28-30

My Time with God

Walk by faith and not by sight.
2 Corinthians 5:7

My Time with God

If God be for me, who can be against me?
Romans 8:31

Chapter 2: Counseling Helps Piece the Puzzle Together

I have worked in the medical field for 19 years now. I started in the field as a certified nursing assistant (CNA) and later became a Certified Medical Assistant (CMA) and am working on a Masters in health and wellness management. Therefore, being in the field this long I have seen so much growth and advances in the way procedure and surgeries are performed, and the advances in technology. With that being said, I know first-hand there are other alternatives to experiencing motherhood. Alternative options include surrogacy, and egg or sperm donation, the use of fertility drugs, intrauterine insemination (IUI), in vitro fertilization (IVF), and adoption. These alternatives can provide hope for starting a family, As a medical professional these are options that we speak to families about, looking to give them hope in one day starting a family, but from a patient this makes me feel sad because I didn't want to be offered these options, not because I thought I was too good for surrogacy or any of the other options, but during this time I was stuck in an angry place and self-pity; still feeling like life was so unfair because my soon to be ex-husband was able to have a baby outside the marriage and yet I wasn't able to conceive during the marriage or after. However, surrogacy is an arrangement, often supported by a legal document, whereby a woman agrees to deliver/labor a baby for another woman or family, who will become the child's parent after birth. Furthermore, before choosing any alternatives on your journey to fertility, it is important to have a support system in place. There will be big decisions that you will have to make on this journey, and it is easier to make these decisions and go through the journey if you speak with a counselor or have some type of support system in place.

Counseling and support from a fertility specialists can help you find the best treatment for yourself, take care of your mental health, and get through this difficult time in your life. Joining a support group and getting a health and fertility coach can help you to remain calm and focus on strategies to successfully cope with infertility. The physical, emotional, and social effects of infertility can be overwhelming and have a significant impact on a woman's mental and emotional well-being. The good news is that there are several counseling options available to infertile women that can help them cope with the trials of infertility and support them on their journey to conception. One option for infertile women is to see a reproductive endocrinologist. These specialists are trained in diagnosing and treating infertility and can provide a variety of options including in-vitro fertilization (IVF) and other assisted reproductive technologies (ARTs) to help couples conceive. They can also provide guidance and support throughout the process, including discussing the risks and benefits of different treatments and helping couples make informed decisions about their care. Another option for infertile women is, to seek counseling from reproductive therapist. These professionals are trained to provide emotional support and guidance to couples dealing with infertility. They can help couples work through their feelings of loss, disappointment, frustration, and provide strategies for coping with the stress and uncertainty of infertility treatment. Support groups can also be a valuable resource for infertile women. Joining a support group can provide emotional support and a sense of community for infertile women. Also, it can be a great way to connect with others who are going through similar experiences, share information and resources. Mental health professionals such as counselors or therapists can be of significant help. They can provide counseling or therapy to help infertile women cope with the mental impact of infertility by working through feelings of depression, anxiety, and stress. They can also help couples improve communication and strengthen their relationship during this challenging time. It is important to remember that infertility is a complex and personal issue, and each woman's experience will be unique. Infertile women need to discuss their options with their healthcare provider and find the type of counseling that works best for them. With the right support, infertile women can find the strength and resilience to navigate the challenge of infertility and achieve their dream of becoming parents.

I know first-hand how effective counseling can be when dealing with tough situations such as divorce and infertility. I was seeing a divorce counselor, who suggested I join a grief and anger support group. Which I did, and utilizing both services were highly effective in managing the mental and emotional stress that I was dealing with from the divorce and infertility struggles. I remember my first night sitting in a circle at the support group and listening to others share their stories, as it became my turn to share my story, I had a big meltdown. It was the first time I had shared everything I was going through. With so much rage and anger I shared how I felt like I was being punished for something and didn't understand why I was going through so much pain. But the love, support, and prayers that was poured on me that night from so many strangers, was something that I had never felt. I met this young lady that night, who was pregnant at the time; as she leaned in to hug me and console me, she whispered to me these words "you will become a mom the doctors cannot determine your end, God wrote your ending before your beginning, only he knows what's waiting ahead for you." I was told I wouldn't have more kids but here I am pregnant with my third, she said. If God can bless me and I know I haven't all ways done what's right, I know he will open your womb and bless you too, she said. She continued sharing her story and before I knew it, we ended up talking all night, realizing the group session ran overtime by an hour or two. We were so caught up in sharing stories, but most of all sharing about the goodness of the Lord. God knew I was going to withstand and come out victorious, just like he knows the same for you! I didn't know any of these people in the support group, it was our first-time meeting but, yet I felt so close to them, felt as if I had known them all my life. That night these strangers became family. From that day on I could not wait for the nights we would meet for our sessions. I felt as if I got stronger and stronger each session and was able to better deal with my mental and emotional health. God has not forgotten you. He sees your tears and understands your pain. What I learned that was not from the words that were shared, but from the examples I saw in the room. Everyone had gone through something, survived, and triumphed over whatever it was that they thought was going to take them out. Here's the thing I learned; what they went through was not meant to destroy them, it was for someone else, it was meant to be used to help someone else heal from the same struggle or issue; just like what I am doing now. God choose you for this battle because he knows that you are strong enough to handle it. Being barring wasn't meant for me to become defeated and not reproduce in the body, it was meant to build my faith and help others triumph over their struggles and issues with infertility. I'm so grateful for the individuals I met that night. To this day we are still close. I recalled 19 days after my daughter was born, my mom was diagnosed with breast cancer and while I became the care giver for my mom, these same individuals pulled together, and helped me with my daughter and mom. However, I never would have met such blessings if I didn't take my counselor advice and join a support group. God work in mysterious ways but moves so strategically. He rarely uses those around you or those that you have been a blessing to, to bless you. He will send complete strangers your way to be a blessing in your life. Allow God to build your circle and your life will be forever blessed.

Furthermore, a person does not have to provide physical and/or financial assistance to show their support. A lot of people forget that showing kindness, empathy and compassion is a way we can show support for one another. This reminds me of the time when I first found out my husband had walked out on me because he had got another woman pregnant. I was devastated, alone, hopeless, and felt betrayed. I felt as if I didn't have anybody.

However, it was at this moment that God used my brother to minister to me and remind me that in life a simple check-in can go way further than some one giving me monetary or physical help. Going through a divorce is tough on its own but going through a divorce because of infertility is another level of difficulty. Even, though I didn't have the physical or financial help that I thought I needed, God came through in a different way. He spoke to me through a text message my brother sent me. To this day those words are forever in my heart. They remind me of my strength and that, what is for me is for me, and I don't need to become or look like someone else to get my blessing. It's going to happen, just in God's timing. The message from my brother read, "baby girl, I'm sorry that you are experiencing so much pain and having to go through this difficult situation. I want to tell you that you are stronger than me I could not have survived all you have gone through and now a divorce. God know who to give certain battles to because he knows who is strong enough to handle them. You have strength like no other. I want to let you know that you are beautiful, you will be a great mother one day. I see how you are with your nephew. God going to bless you with a man that will love you for you and not going to care about your body size and if you can't have kids; all he's going to see is the beautiful, strong, God loving woman you are. If he doesn't, he's not the one for you. I wish I could take the pain for you. I hate you are going through all of this over there by yourself. Just know I love you with my whole life." This message came right on time, and it did more for me than any materialistic help could have. We often forget how powerful words can be. Life and death live in the words we speak. My brother probably didn't realize that he was speaking life over me. I started to say a prayer from this message, asking God to help me to see me the way he sees me and to send the man that he is preparing for me. That man that will love all of me, infertility, being a heavy girl, and all that were to come with me. God did just that he sent the exact Guy my brother said that he would bless me with. I didn't have to change anything about me, and he wasn't at all concerned about not being able to have a baby, and he accepted everything that came with me. He didn't fold at the first sight of pressure. But I don't think I would have gotten to that place if my brother had not shown me support and love through a simple check-in. Prior to that message, I had given up hope and was ready to throw in the towel on life. This really helped to build my faith. What I want you to learn here is there will be times in life that

God not going to send physical help but he's going to send you a word. Why? Because his word says in Roman 10:17, faith comes by hearing, and hearing of the word of God.

Prayer: God, I thank you for even the trials I am going through. I know it seems tough now but, yet I know I will come out on top, and you will get the glory. Holy spirit I ask that you guide me to the right counselors. Build my community of support and supporters, that will help me ease the hurt and pain, so I can pour back into others as God has poured back into me. God, I thank you in advance for my victory, healing, and deliverance. For this too shall pass and I know the pain is temporary, it has not come to stay. I am whole, I am healed, and I will now go and be about my father's business. In Jesus name Amen, Amen, and Amen!

Self-Reflection Questions

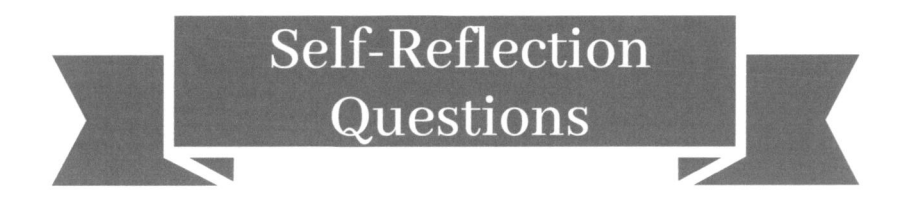

1. What have you done in the past to cope with the challenges of life? Was this helpful?_____
_____
_____
_____
_____
_____

2. Have you ever thought about seeking counseling or joining a support group(s) to help you get through life challenges? Why or why not?_____
_____
_____
_____
_____
_____

3. List 3 support groups that you are thinking about joining. Do these support groups offer in person or virtual visits? Why do you want to join these groups?_____
_____
_____
_____
_____

My Time with God

Write the vision and make it plain.
Habakkuk 2:2

My Time with God

**Faith without work is dead.
James 2:26**

My Time with God

The Lord is my shepherd; I shall not want.
Psalms 23

Chapter 3: Forgiveness Make Room for Blessings

Forgiveness affects the whole person; mentally, physically, and emotionally. The more you rest on unforgiveness the more you hold yourself captive to negative thoughts and emotions. An unforgiving heart gives the enemy easy access to your mind and feelings, causing a person to become bitter, restless, depressed, isolated, and lose self-worth. I had to practice the act of forgiving myself because I became angry, depressed, and isolated. I was mad at the world, especially with every woman that passed me with a child. I would often time ask God why me? Why my body was not normal? Why I could not be the woman to give my husband a child? I would question myself and God almost daily. I just needed to know what I did wrong, what I could have done differently, or what I did and did not do after each situation where I experienced loss, such as with the divorce, and both miscarriages. The first time I learned about the power of forgiveness was in 2013 when I went through a tough divorce. The day I went to court was the first time I had seen my husband in 6 months. He left me on New Year's 2013 with no explanation or answers. I did not know if he was going to be gone for days, weeks, months, years, and or forever. I found out from a neighbor that my husband had left. When I got home my neighbor said to me "is everything okay?" I saw your husband packing his car and all he said to me was "hi" while continuing to pack his car. I walked into the house, and everything was gone as if my house was robbed of all my husband's things. Days, weeks, and months go by, and there were no words from him. After the fifth month and no words, phone calls, or texts, and not knowing where my husband was, I did the only thing I felt I could do. I filed for divorce. I never knew you could feel a broken heart until I felt the pain in my heart and stomach every time, I thought of him and the situation. Day in and day out I would pray for answers. One day my cousin, God-sister, and neighbor gathered at my house to check in on me and there I lie on the couch in tears. I still had no way of communicating with him, not sure if he was ok, or knowing what I had done wrong. At that point they all looked at me and said in unison "a man doesn't just up and leave, there had to be a reason." Then my neighbor looks at me and said, "Stacy, I'm sorry to say this, but men that leave the way he did only leaves for 1 reason, possibly a child." The first time I ever gave that idea a thought. That was the most hurtful truth I ever heard. I replied "please" do not say that as my heart was dropping to my feet. I did not want to believe that could be the reason, because I was a barren woman. I cried the hardest lying in my cousin's arms. I told them I do not know if I could ever make it through this, especially if I find that to be the reason for him leaving. The day before we got married the doctor told us that I would never be able to have kids. After a year into the marriage, I started seeing the doctors more because I was trying to have a baby, and nothing was working. PCOS was taking control of my body and my cycles were becoming more irregular. God, why me? I begged and pleaded. Asking God to take away the pain and bring my husband back and for that to not be the reason he left. I looked him in the face for the first time at our court hearing and asked, why did you leave? The answer I got was so cold and heartless. He looked at me and responded with, I do not know, I love you, but this is just something I had to do. Weeks before the divorce decree came in the mail, I found out from social media that my husband was having a baby and engaged to marry this woman, which he did marry after our divorce was final. At that moment my heart stopped beating, I could not breathe, and I felt like life was over. I was still a barren woman and became so angry with God. I kept saying God how could this be? Why is this happening to me? He knew how much having a baby, and being a mom meant to me. But he just had to be unfaithful and get another woman pregnant while married to me. At that very moment that was the lowest I ever felt. I did not feel like a woman anymore since I could not do the one thing that God created women bodies to do, and that is to carry a child and bring forth life. Years went by and I was still grieving the divorce. At that moment I knew I had unforgiveness in my heart. My relationship with my now husband started rocky because I was bringing all the hurt and pain from the previous marriage into the relationship. It was clear I still had forgiving to do before this relationship could be successful. 3 years later my ex-husband reached out to me to speak his peace.

    What he had to say did not matter to me at the time because I was more focused on what I needed to say. At that very moment, I realized that forgiveness was not for him but for me. I spoke my mind, shed my tears, and ended the call with I forgive you. However, I am still hurting and still trying to figure out how to heal from all this. I still cannot have a baby. With so much pain and hurt in my voice, I told him that it is time for him to forgive himself for the mistakes he made and the pain he caused, so, he can be the best father he could be to his daughter. After that conversation, I instantly went to work on my healing. I knew I had truly forgiven my ex-husband when I was able to speak with my current husband about our options to have children and marriage. God could not bless me in my mess. I had to clean some things on the inside of me and purge all the things that were holding me back. God had to isolate me and peel off one layer at a time. I didn't realize at the time that forgiving him made room in my heart and life to enjoy the bountiful blessings that were coming my way. The other time I experienced forgiveness was during the loss of my 3rd baby. One day I was out shopping for onesies for my daughter. One month had passed since I suffered an ectopic pregnancy. My body was still sore from surgery. A stranger walked up to me and asked if I thought she was crazy with tears in her eyes. I started to look around because I wasn't sure if she was speaking to me. I thought this was a prank. Once I realized she was serious and was speaking to me, I replied why would I think you crazy? I do not know you. She answered, I just lost a baby, and my husband thinks I should be over it by now, but here I am in the baby section looking at clothes and I have no baby to buy for. At that moment God not only help this lady through me but helped me as well. I grabbed her hand and said to her, "no", I do not think you are crazy. What I do think is, you are grieving, and I feel your pain. I understand your pain, and I am your pain. I just lost a baby and my fallopian tube; a month ago, and I still cry, have meltdowns, and get frustrated; especially at my husband. However, it's okay to cry and grieve; you just don't want to stay in that season too long. To help you get through this season you first must give yourself grace and know that this did not happen because of something you did or did not do. Forgive yourself so you can free yourself from that guilt that is weighing on you mentally and emotionally. Next, forgive your husband. He is only saying these things because he is hurting and grieving as well. Hurt people, hurt people. Lastly, no one can tell you how long to grieve I told her. I asked if she believe in God and prayer, and she responded I do. I went on to tell her to ask God for comfort, strength, peace, and forgiveness, so, she can start her journey to healing. The same advice I gave this stranger, God used to minister to me because, I too was upset with my husband. I went home and apologized to my husband for being so mean to him for grieving differently. This encounter with this young lady taught me how to give grace, be kind, and be loving to myself and my husband no matter what the situation looks like; because what it feels like is not what it truly is. God's word says to be kind to each other, tenderhearted, and forgiving one another, just as God has forgiven you because you belong to Christ (Ephesians 4:32).

One thing this life has taught me is: you can't change the past; you can only live in the now and look forward to tomorrow. So, why not forgive? Not forgiving will not change anything. It will not undo what was done. Therefore, bring peace and joy back to your life by practicing the act of forgiveness.

Prayer: Father, I thank you for your love and support through this challenging time. Father if you search my heart and find unforgiveness, clean me, wash me, and make me whole. So, I too may have a forgiving heart to forgive myself and others as you do me. I do not want to feel this pain anymore. For this person and situation has caused me so much hurt and pain, I lay it all down at your feet and when I am done praying, God I am releasing and walking away from everything that does not serve me in the way that is pleasing to you. In Jesus's name Amen, Amen, Amen!

Self-Reflection Questions

1. What are the things or people in your life that you need to forgive? _____
_____
_____
_____
_____
_____

2. Why are you holding on to the thing(s) that caused you so much pain? Explain. _____
_____
_____
_____
_____
_____

3. Explain what you could have done to change the outcome or situation? Do you think doing this would have made a difference? Why or why not? Explain. _____
_____
_____
_____
_____
_____

My Time with God

Greater is he that is in me.
1 John 4:4

My Time with God

I can do all things through Christ!
Philippians 4:13

My Time with God

No weapon that is formed shall prosper.
Isaiah 54:17

Chapter 4: Gratitude is Contagious

Another principle I learned to apply on this journey is, gratitude. Once I learned the power of being grateful for the things that were around me, I was able to see that I did not have time to waste on self-pity, doubt, or fear. I had to place my thoughts on things that were good and pleasing to God. The things that were intended for my good. You see, often time we get caught up in the fear of the unknown that we cannot see the good and known that is in plain view every day. This remind me of a conversation I had with my god-mom. Every morning I would call my God mom for daily prayer. She would always answer the phone "Good morning beautiful." One day I asked, why did you say that? She replied, every morning I wake up I look in the mirror and say "good morning beautiful" to the woman staring back at me. She would smile and go on to have a good day she says. You determine how your day is going to be, and I choose to have a beautiful, grateful, and productive day. Then one day it hit me she explained, to say it to other women, because you never know how someone's day has started and that maybe the only time that they may hear or be reminded of how beautiful they are. It sets the tone for my day, she declared, so why not set the tone for others? She continued to say, it is a blessing to be a blessing. The next day I tried it. I woke up and said, "good morning beautiful" and as a natural response I replied with a smile "good morning." I did the same routine the next day and the next for about a week. By the time I got to the second week, I was still saying "good morning beautiful." Doing this every morning allowed me to set the tone for my day. This daily practice led me to give thanks to my heavenly father but also embedding a spirit of gratitude in my heart. In life some things bring so much peace, it makes you look forward to seeing another day. That is what this morning routine did for me. I then found myself looking forward to the next day so I could have that powerful conversation with myself. My God-mom was right, it was the only time I would hear you're beautiful, and any other quality I possessed. I had to remind myself that, "the same thing you want others to see in you, you first have to see them in yourself." As the song says, "sometimes we have to encourage ourselves, no matter how we are feeling." Speaking life over yourself will aid in your healing, manifestation, releasing and transformation. From then on, I woke up every morning just to give God a "thank you!" A thank you for the simple things in life. The things we often time take for granted; like a sound mind, breath in our bodies, peace, keeping us through the night, giving traveling grace and mercy throughout the day, and so on. Having a grateful heart pushed me to enjoy the life that I was blessed to have. The next minute, hour, second, or day is not promised, so take time daily to find something to be thankful for. Practicing gratitude allowed me to enjoy the kids that were in my life. I stop worrying about the possibility of never becoming a mom and started thanking God for the mother spirit and anointing that was in me. This allowed me to care for and love on the children that he had placed in my life.

To all those that are going through infertility, just know you are not alone. I know it can be a lonely and scary journey, but it's a battle you can win. You have already won. Look around you and count your wins. I was once scared too. Scared of the unknown or the uncomfortableness that we may experience from the unknown outcome. Therefore, I boldly encourage you to not be afraid of the unknown but to be open to the possibilities that may come your way. God blesses us in ways that we least expect. We must be open to receive. God promise that he will never leave or forsake us. He knows what we are going through. He knows that we are scared but you must dig deep and pull out whatever little hope and faith that lies within you. You can and you will succeed. Success is in your DNA. You were not created to fail, to be fearful, to be inferior, defeated, and or to be a victim. God created you for greatness, to prosper, to be victorious, bold, and to conquer. At the end of the day, you will win and come out victorious!

No one can tell you what your win will look like or how it should look, only God knows that. But in due season he will reveal it to you. Continue to be grateful and happy on purpose. By recognizing that there are things in your life to be grateful for. Lastly, I want to remind you that your fears and worries about the unknown are irrelevant and do not deserve your time and attention. They will not help you grow. They will keep and leave you stuck in misery.

 I would like to share this simple exercise that I do every day. It's not something that I do at a specific time of the day but when my heart lead me to do it, I do it. Now that I have a family my husband have us to do this little exercise before leaving home or soon as we enter the car. The exercise is simple, all you have to do is name 10 things that you are thankful for and that's it. Try this for a week and see how you feel. It will change your thinking and appreciation, even for the small things in life. We have made this into a daily practice and trust me if we go a day without engaging in this exercise our day is thrown off.

 I enjoy this exercise because it taught me

something about myself. I no longer waste time focusing on what I don't have, what's not going right in my life, what's missing, what's needed and what's wanted. Focusing on what's missing, will only have you seeing the small picture and you will never be able to bring yourself to see the big picture, see what God has done for you thus for, or to be able to build your faith and believe that you can have everything that has been promised to you. God plans for us to be successful and to live the abundant and fulfilled life. We can't carry out God's plan if we get stuck or tricked into focusing on what's missing or what we are lacking. If we dwell on what we don't have, we will then always not have because we have fixed our eyes to only see the problem and not the solution. Seeing the solution allows us to put our plan into motion and create the life or results we desire, and God planned!

    I am so thankful that I didn't allow myself to stay in the space where I was only able to see all the wrong that was happening. Like, my husband walking out on me, not having a job, not being able to produce in my body, and the list go on but the point I am making is because I figured out how to rise above the problems by focusing my time and energy on the things I do have I was able to work through the problems. I got a better job, a better husband, and the ability to produce in my body. Sitting back dwelling on failures, past hurt, and pains can cause us to box God and ourselves in. When God wants you to live free. It's time to come out the box and expand your mind.

Prayer: Father, I boldly come to you and thank you for all the many blessings that you have surrounded me with. I thank you for the love, friendships, and children that you have placed in my life. Forgive me father for all the times I took my eyes off the good things surrounding me and chose to place my heart and eyes on worry, fear, and lack. I am beautiful, I am fearlessly, and wonderfully made and thank you for taking the time to create an imperfectly perfect person like me. Help me to keep my mind stayed on things that are good and when doubt, fear, or anything that is not of you and don't serve me purpose, tries to creep in; just know I will continue to be grateful. In Jesus's name Amen, Amen, and Amen!

Self-Reflection Questions

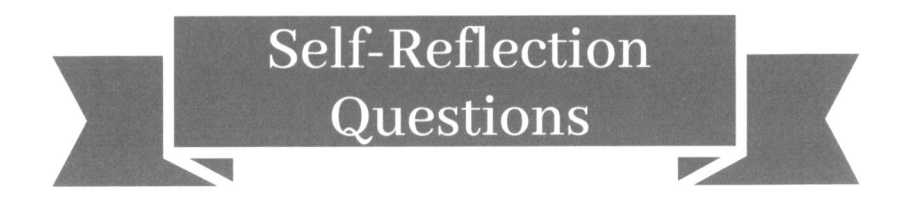

1. Look around you, list 3 things for which you are grateful. Why are you grateful for these things? _____
_____
_____
_____
_____
_____

2. What are some things in your life that you are taking for granted, that you can be thankful for?_____
_____
_____
_____
_____
_____

3. What life experiences (good or bad) have you had that you are grateful for? What did you learn from them? _____
_____
_____
_____
_____
_____

My Time with God

Rejoice evermore and pray without ceasing.
1 Thessalonians 5:16–17

My Time with God

O give thanks unto the Lord for he is good!
Psalm 107:1

My Time with God

Every good and perfect gift is from above.
James 1:17

Chapter 5: Weight Loss is a Must

Being overweight has always been an issue for me. I was born with asthma; therefore, I had been on steroid medication all my life. Causing me to be heavy as a child. As old people say I was just big boned. Then came the diagnosis of Poly Cystic Ovarian Syndrome, known as (PCOS). I did not know what this condition was nor how to treat it. However, the only thing the doctor explained to me was that there was no cure, and I can manage my symptoms with diet and exercise. "Really," I said to myself. I was trying to figure out how that was going to be possible. Being that I am taking medication to treat asthma; that's causing weight gain. I felt lost and didn't think it was possible. Time went on and I wanted to be a mom and PCOS was out of control. I went back to see the doctor and she said, "Your weight plays a key role in getting pregnant."

Being under or overweight can affect your ability to get pregnant or cause problems while pregnant. For me the inability to get pregnant was caused from being overweight. The weight gain was caused by steroid medication and by Poly Cystic Ovarian Syndrome (PCOS) which is a condition that causes hormonal imbalances, leading to weight gain. Not only was it hard to lose weight but it felt impossible also, to lose weight. I was always stressed and frustrated. At times I found myself emotionally eating and not eating, depending on the stressor at the time. However, emotionally eating and not eating are both bad for the body. When you emotionally eat, you overeat and majority of the time you are indulging in unhealthy items that are high in sugars, carbs, and unhealthy fats. When you emotionally do not eat, you are placing your body in starvation mode. which in return causes your body to store food as fat. This means your body is not breaking the food down and releasing it for energy. PCOS does not just affect a person physically, it affects the whole person. The mind, body, and spirit. I became moody, depressed, obese, financially, and spiritually depleted, while dealing with PCOS. I was letting my emotions get the best of me all the time. One day while reading my bible I was led to the scripture that says, Human beings cannot live on bread alone, but need every word that God speaks (Matthew 4:4). This scripture reminded me that I was a whole being and not a partial being. That I had to take care of the whole person to see results. Mind, Spirit, and Body. I had to remove doubt and fear from my mind, by staying in my word through meditation and prayer, and physically move my body through exercise. I had to change my diet as well. Once I started to focus on the whole person, I was able to lose the extra weight, better manage my stress levels and the stressors that were causing stress. I had to shift the way I thought about food, my health, and my body. I invested in a personal trainer, develop better eating habits, got better control of my cycles, and 4 years later I gave birth to a healthy baby girl! "Yay!" I did it, mission accomplish, at least that is what I thought until life threw me a curve ball 19 days after my daughter was born. My mom was diagnosed with breast cancer. Now,

I have this newborn and my mom to care for, and my mental health is all over the place. Therefore, my priorities shifted. Just like that a new stressor came in and threw everything off balance. I was no longer focusing on my mind, body, or spirit. The cycle of irregular cycles started over, PCOS out of control again, and I am now heavier than I've ever been. Now I am battling with PCOS, High blood pressure, a 14-month-old baby, my mom and her cancer. I felt the weight of the world just pressing on me again. I didn't think it could get any worse, but it did. I find out I'm 8+ weeks pregnant and the baby is growing in my tubes… I was then rushed to emergency surgery to remove the baby. All went well with the surgery and now it's time for a follow-up. This visit changed my life forever. Doctors informed me that PCOS was out of control and now I'm a diabetic and to add I had developed liver disease. A fatty liver is what they call it. The only option I was given at the time was to have a hysterectomy. My doctor said it's the only option. It would help with the hormones being unbalanced, also to continue to take the diabetic medicine because it will aid in the weight loss and then diet and exercise. Well, I learned my lesson early on after getting pregnant with my daughter; not to make decisions without consulting God first. I did that before I was pregnant with Mireya. I was scheduled for preop to get a hysterectomy when I found out I was pregnant with my daughter. I chose at the time a hysterectomy because I believed the doctors when they said I would never have kids. Now, I just lost a baby, and they are still giving me the same option. I went home and spent time praying. I meditated on Luke10:19 Listen! I have given you authority, so that you can walk on snakes and scorpions and overcome all the power of the Enemy, and nothing will hurt you (GNT). I wrote this scripture on a sticky note and stuck it to my bathroom mirror. Every time I went to the bathroom, I read this scripture. It reminded me that I had the authority to change my life and I did not have to stay stuck in the place I was in, and that nothing the doctors were saying, was going to win. I was in control of my outcome, I just needed to stand firm on my beliefs and not make permanent decisions based off temporary feelings. My aunt taught me this scripture early on in life and told me it was her favorite. She also told me to keep this scripture close to heart; saying that it would help me in time of troubles and uncertainties. And when all my hope was gone; this scripture did just that. After constantly seeking God for guidance, I followed-up with my medical provider 2 weeks later and asked him to be honest with me. I explained how I know God is going to bless me with more babies and getting a hysterectomy does not sit well with my spirit. He looked at me and replied I know you want more babies but if you don't lose a significant amount of weight fast, you're going to have non-alcoholic cirrhosis of the liver.

However, losing a significant amount of weight can reverse it. From the knowledge and experience, I gained from working in the medical field. I knew I didn't want to be a liver patient. Thus, I looked at my doctor and said, "Doc" give it to me straight what are my options. I am not getting a hysterectomy if all I need to do is lose weight. He then looked at my record and said, "what happen," you lost weight and then gained it all back. What did you do to lose weight the first time? He asked. I gave him the side eye and answered. I had a trainer but with PCOS, I was wasting money. The weight came off and came right back. He chuckled, and said, "okay, given your history with PCOS, diabetes, high blood pressure, and obesity, you are the perfect candidate for the sleeve." I laughed and said, "Sleeve it is!" I know you're probably thinking sleeve, what is that? Simply put, a gastric sleeve is a surgical procedure that involves removing the larger portion of the stomach. So, I got the sleeve, and it was by far the hardest, but best decision I ever made. The ectopic pregnancy and sleeve saved my life. The enemy tried to use everything he could to break me, but God used it all for my good and saved me. If I had to do it all over again I would. In 2019, I was 235 pounds when I was sleeved. I am currently down 100 pounds and maintaining. I constantly pray and meditate, I made simple lifestyle changes, by exercising daily, even if it's a 15-minute walk, and eat a vegetarian/plant-based diet. But I do not deprive myself. I was forced to change my relationship with food. The sleeve forced me to go on a sabbatical from all the unhealthy food that brings us comfort but makes us feel so bad. What people don't understand is, we don't know when we are in an unhealthy relationship until our lives are on the line. By time we realize we are in an unhealthy situation, sometimes it is then too late to make a change. So, make up your mind today to make a change!

Prayer: Father, I thank you for the body that you have blessed me with. I ask for your guidance on this weight loss journey. Help me to see me, as you see me. Help me to think of myself, as you think of me, for I am worthy, I am enough, I am beautiful. Lastly, father, mold me and shape me to your liking. I know losing this weight isn't going to be easy, but my life is worth the effort I will have to put in, to live the life you have plan for me. With your grace and guidance, I can do anything because all things are possible to him who believes, and I believe in you and me. In Jesus's name Amen!

Self-Reflection Questions

1. Knowing your why is important in reaching any goal. Why do you want to lose weight? _____
_____
_____
_____
_____
_____

2. How much weight do you want to lose? What is your plan of action (your how)? _____
_____
_____
_____
_____
_____

3. What life experiences (good or bad) have you had that you are grateful for? What did you learn from them? _____
_____
_____
_____
_____
_____

My Time with God

Love your enemies! Do good to them.
Luke 6:35

My Time with God

Your Body is a temple, given to you by God.
Corinthians 6:19

My Time with God

Whatever you do, do all to the glory of God.
1 Corinthians 10:31

Chapter 6: It Did Not Happen Overnight

In life we expect change to take place suddenly, often times forgetting that change occurs in stages and cycles. Take the birthing process for example, you don't just wake up and magically become pregnant and ready to give birth. It's a process that you must go through before the woman is ready to deliver. First, a woman and man must engage in unprotected intercourse; during this time the woman body will release the egg for a man semen to fertilize, then conception occurs, and the baby grows in the woman womb for the next 9 months. At 40 week the woman is then ready to give birth. Well, the same goes for other areas of our lives. Especially, if we are looking to make a change physically, spiritually, emotionally, mentally, or financially. We must give ourselves grace. We didn't become broken, financially broke, or unhealthy in our bodies overnight. This was a process that took time to form. A process commonly known as a habit. As busy individuals we create routines and or behaviors patterns that get stuck on replay, forcing us to create a memory of this behavior in the subconscious mind making it easier to engage in such activity without even thinking hard about it. The subconscious is your true self. It's the part of the mind that we don't see. It houses our beliefs, emotions, habits, values, long-term memory, and imagination. Sigmund Freud uses the iceberg analogy to describe the conscious and the subconscious. The least working part of the mind is, the conscious mind. It uses about 10% of the brain, which is the tip of the iceberg, the thing you can see. But the part of the iceberg that can't be seen, the part under the water is the largest. This is referred to as the subconscious mind using about 90% of the brain. The subconscious is working without us knowing it is working. It influences your actions and feelings. Depending on where you are in your life, your subconscious mind can become your best friend or worst enemy. If you are in a place where you feel all hope is gone and you can't see your way out, then your subconscious mind is going to control you in a negative way, allowing you to continue to partake in negative behaviors that will lead to self-destruction. Furthermore, the subconscious mind can yet become your best friend, if you let it.

    Your subconscious has power over your behaviors, both negative and positive. Therefore, we can create the life we want, by training our brain to produce more positive behaviors. We must remember, you did not get this way overnight. It takes 21 days to create a habit, therefore, it will take you just as long to break that habit. And that's what I had to tell myself. It was hard getting my health on the right track. After getting the sleeve I remember standing in the mirror asking, myself, how did I get like this? What took place in my life, causing me to let go of myself? Asking myself those questions allowed me to tap into the subconscious and replay activities or routines I created, so when I found myself in that situation, I could challenge those familiar and unhealthy thoughts, feelings, and surroundings with a positive. I started taking things one day at a time, it's true what they say, Rome wasn't built overnight. I gave myself grace on days where I didn't think I could make the mark. Reinforcing all the things I had done right. "You are not a programed robot. Things will not be perfect, but the more you try, the more you will improve, is what I told myself."

The first thing to understand in breaking habits is, to start small. Just like it took me time and uncontrolled situations to put the weight on, it was going to take me time to get it off. The first habit I had to break was to stop looking in the mirror and not liking what I saw. To change that I spent the next 30 days or so looking in the mirror and speaking positively to the person that was looking back at me; until it became a habit and a belief. The bible teaches us that we are what we think, therefore, I had to make sure my thinking, speaking, hearing, and seeing became aligned to where I was trying to go. Another important step I took to transform my health and body was finding what made me happy. I had to take the happy or good feeling that I associated with food and other unhealthy substances and start to place those feelings on things that I couldn't eat or drink. For example, I found that being outdoors on the walking trails made me so happy and brought so much peace, that when I started to crave those unhealthy items that provided that good feeling, I would go for a walk and spend time with self and God. The more I did this practice the more I started to have understanding and guidance as to where I was going in life, all while shedding pounds.

    Needless to say, I pray that whatever you are dealing with in life, you understand it's not permanent. Pain is temporary, the bible says we shall suffer for a little while. It's all happening for a reason and a season. With proper guidance, being in the right position, and having the willingness to accept change, you can turn any situation around. You are not meant to stay infertile; you are created to be prosperous and live an abundant fulfilled life. Whatever it is, whether you are working to lose weight, get healthy, increase your finances, become debt free, finish school, buy your dream home, start a family, or whatever, remember you didn't get to this low point overnight, there were some repetitive behaviors you participated in and over time you got to this place. Now, it's time to reverse the cycle of a downward spiral by participating in positive behaviors that will ultimately create good habits, thrusting you closer to living your dream life. It's time to train the subconscious mind to build you up and not tear you down. Give yourself grace and start today to take back your life and power!

Prayer: Father, I thank you for creating me to have life more abundantly and giving me the ability to have what I say. I know I didn't get here overnight but with your grace, mercy, and guidance I am confident that I will be successful in achieving my goals. I thank you father that your will is my life and when I fall off track that you will forgive me, have mercy upon me, and lead me back to the path of righteous night. I

I know this road won't be easy, but it will be worth it, for I am worth it, I am enough, I am strong, I am willful, I am blessed, I am favored, I am healthy, I am yours, and my answer will forever be a yes and amen. In Jesus name amen, amen, and amen!

Self-Reflection Questions

1. Now that you know that change happens in stages and phases, what do dislike and like about the change that's taking place in your life? _____
_____
_____
_____
_____
_____

2. What are the benefits of having this change to come to pass?
_____
_____
_____
_____
_____
_____

3. What will help you to prepare for this change?_____
_____
_____
_____
_____
_____
_____

My Time with God

Whatever you ask in prayer, you will receive.
Matthew 21:22

My Time with God

Old things passes away; all things become new.
2 Corinthians 5:17

My Time with God

There is a time and season for everything.
Ecclesiastes 3:1-8

Bonuses

The bonus includes the action steps that I took to get my life and health in order. Before you can begin to make change, you must first make up your mind you want to change. Next, you must do self-inventory to determine in what area change is necessary. Third, create an action plan that you can stick to and achieve in the desired amount of time you want to achieve it. A valuable tool to use is the SMART goal worksheet. Lastly, you just need to start. There will never be the perfect time to start making change. Something will always come up or distract you. Push through and start even if it means starting small and simple, just start!

Here is an example of how the process look for me.
1. I needed to seek counseling and guidance to get through so much hurt and pain. But most importantly to shift my mindset.

2. I had to track unhealthy behaviors. So, I could know what unhealthy behavior I was engaging in unknowingly.

3. I then downloaded my fitness pal app to make sure I was staying on track with working out and eating healthy (accountability partner)

4. I acted by, using my SMART Goal tool and meal tracker. I was able to create a plan that was easy to maintain, even on days where I got distracted.

5. I had to start thinking, seeing, and speaking positively over my life daily. Using my daily affirmations.

Instructions

The meal tracker on the next page will be your guide to tracking eating habits for the next 14 days; that is, if your impossible situation is to lose weight. After 14 days of tracking your meals if you notice unhealthy items that you can take out your diet do so now, by starting small taking away 1 item at a time. Then download my fitness pal app and start counting calories. The app will tell you the number of calories you need daily after you answer simple questions (i.e., age, height, and weight). Then create your action plan using the SMART Goal chart. Third, use the 14-day affirmation to shift your speaking and your mindset positively. Lastly, you can create your own affirmations if you would like to continue on this Journey.

Weekly Meal Tracker

WEEK OF :

MONTH :

MONDAY
Breakfast	
Lunch	
Dinner	
Snack	

TUESDAY
Breakfast	
Lunch	
Dinner	
Snack	

WEDNESDAY
Breakfast	
Lunch	
Dinner	
Snack	

THURSDAY
Breakfast	
Lunch	
Dinner	
Snack	

FRIDAY
Breakfast	
Lunch	
Dinner	
Snack	

SATURDAY
Breakfast	
Lunch	
Dinner	
Snack	

SUNDAY
Breakfast	
Lunch	
Dinner	
Snack	

WATER INTAKE :

Monday	🥛	🥛	🥛	🥛	🥛	🥛	🥛	🥛
Tuesday	🥛	🥛	🥛	🥛	🥛	🥛	🥛	🥛
Wednesday	🥛	🥛	🥛	🥛	🥛	🥛	🥛	🥛
Thursday	🥛	🥛	🥛	🥛	🥛	🥛	🥛	🥛
Friday	🥛	🥛	🥛	🥛	🥛	🥛	🥛	🥛
Saturday	🥛	🥛	🥛	🥛	🥛	🥛	🥛	🥛
Sunday	🥛	🥛	🥛	🥛	🥛	🥛	🥛	🥛

Weekly Meal Tracker

WEEK OF :

MONTH :

MONDAY
- Breakfast
- Lunch
- Dinner
- Snack

TUESDAY
- Breakfast
- Lunch
- Dinner
- Snack

WEDNESDAY
- Breakfast
- Lunch
- Dinner
- Snack

THURSDAY
- Breakfast
- Lunch
- Dinner
- Snack

FRIDAY
- Breakfast
- Lunch
- Dinner
- Snack

SATURDAY
- Breakfast
- Lunch
- Dinner
- Snack

SUNDAY
- Breakfast
- Lunch
- Dinner
- Snack

WATER INTAKE :

Monday							
Tuesday							
Wednesday							
Thursday							
Friday							
Saturday							
Sunday							

94

SMART
GOALS

USE THE QUESTIONS BELOW TO CREATE YOUR GOALS. THIS IS YOUR GUIDE TO OVERCOMING ANY IMPOSSIBLE SITUATION THAT HAS ARISEN IN YOUR LIFE. *REMEMBER TO ACHIEVE YOUR DESIRED RESULTS YOU MUST SHOW UP FOR YOURSELF DAILY, BECAUSE NO ONE WILL SHOW UP FOR YOU NOR DO THE WORK FOR YOU* YOU GOT THIS! YOU CAN, AND YOU WILL!

S | **SPECIFIC**
WHAT DO I WANT TO ACCOMPLISH?

M | **MEASURABLE**
HOW WILL I KNOW WHEN IT IS ACCOMPLISHED?

A | **ACHIEVABLE**
HOW CAN THE GOAL BE ACCOMPLISHED? EXPLAIN..

R | **RELEVANT**
DOES THIS SEEM WORTHWHILE? EXPLAIN.

T | **TIME BOUND**
WHEN CAN I ACCOMPLISH THIS GOAL? BE SPECIFIC.

My Vision of Self

Physical

Mental

Spiritual

Emotional

Note

○ Travel

○ Exercise

○ Wishes

2023
Make it Happen Vision Board

Notes :

○ Financial Goal/ Wealth

○ Passion

○ Family

○ Career

○ *Travel*

○ *Exercise*

○ *Wish*

2024
Make it Happen Vision Board

○ *Financial Goal/ Wealth*

Notes :

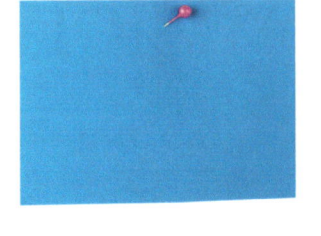

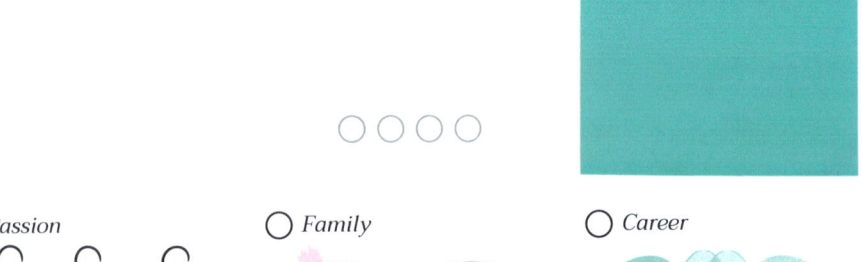

○ *Passion*

○ *Family*

○ *Career*

98

14 DAY AFIRMATIONS

DAY 1: I AM Victorious
· I will not be defeat today or any day to come.

DAY 2: I AM Great
· Greatness is in me, Coming through me, and all around me.

DAY 3: I AM Deserving
· I deserve every good thing that is coming my way. I deserve to live a life with abundance.

DAY 4: I AM Worthy
· I know my worth and can manifest my heart desires. I am open and ready to receive everything good.

DAY 5: I AM Enough
· I don't need to change myself to fit in to be accepted by others.

14 DAY AFFIRMATIONS

DAY 6: I AM Fertile
· I shall reproduce in every area of my life.

DAY 7: I AM a Mother
·I am blessed to be a mother to many.

DAY 8: I AM Resourceful
· I have access to the source that provides the resources.

DAY 9: I AM Powerful
· I will not be influenced or controlled by things that doesn't serve my purpose.

DAY 10: I AM Strong
· I have the ability to withstand the pressures of life.

14 DAY AFFIRMATIONS

DAY 11: I AM a Blessing
· My light will shine bright daily.

Day 12: I AM Healed
· Divine healing is my portion. Every area of my life has been restored.

DAY 13: I AM Whole
· I have been set free from every past hurt, pain, and failure.

DAY 14: I AM Talented
· I have the ability to create the life I so desire.

Notes

Notes

Notes

Notes

Motivation

You can and you will!

Nothing is impossible with GOD!

BEFORE 235LBS

AFTER 145LBS

I DO!

Jan. 22

My FAMILY!

111

BEFORE VS. AFTER

BEFORE VS. AFTER

Apr 2017

Jun 2022

My FOREVER FRIEND!

Let's stay connected!

For Bookings & Speaking Engagements
Email: info.stacybooks@gmail.com
You can follow and tag me on
IG: woman.withpower

Made in the USA
Columbia, SC
12 March 2024